MASTER AND DISCIPLE

by

World Champion
José Luis "Jay-el" Hinojosa, MD

Illustrations
Brett Oberthaler

Also by José Luis "Jay-el" Hinojosa, MD

NOVELS

The Tonic

PLAYS

Rosi Milagros

Chameleon

Exam Room 2

NONFICTION

The Language of Winners!

¡El Lenguaje de los Triunfadores!

Report Card on Rape

Magnets for Health

Tae Kwon Do for Everyone

Frozen in Time

The HELP Secret

SCREENPLAYS

Campeón (co-author)

CONTENTS –

DEDICATION –

I DEDICATE THIS BOOK to my children, José Luis II, Laura Grisel, and Alexis Liset for the never-ending joy they bring to my life.

To Eric, the definition of a true friend.

To my wife, Maria Elena, who fully complements my life.

To my parents, Homero Hinojosa and Rosalinda F. Hinojosa, for all their love and support throughout the years... and may they rest in peace. My mom also taught me a lot of the lessons I share in this book.

To all my dedicatees: I love you.

ACKNOWLEDGMENTS –

I OWE A DEBT OF GRATITUDE to everyone who allowed me to read to them while I was still working on this book.

I thank my son, J.L., who served as talent for the cover design for the 1st edition of *Master and Disciple*... and for this edition he's the talent for the images of the hands found throughout the book. By the way, he recently graduated from Culinary School and he's currently sharing his talents as a Pastry Chef in Texas.

I also thank my friend, Brett Oberthaler, who did a masterful job with the illustrations and drawings included in this book.

Lastly, I'd like to thank my good friend, Professor Silverio Guerra, the Universal Martial Arts Hall of Fame, and the Supreme Sokeship Council for recognizing the positive moral values and lessons contained within *Master and Disciple* and for honoring me with induction into the Hall of Fame in 2008 as *Martial Arts Author of the Year*. I am deeply humbled.

PREFACE –

BELIEVE IT OR NOT, the first few pages of this book were scribbled a few summers ago on a paper napkin, while in the back seat of a crowded car on the way to Disneyland. My good friend, Eric Lee, volunteered to give my children and me the *royal treatment* while on our vacation to California. Since we hadn't been to Disney, he jumped at the opportunity to be a host --- and a great one he was! Personally, I think he was just trying to get away from all those ruthless and tough (or is it toothless and rough?) martial artists who love to train with him.

Surrounded by so much warmth --- yes, it was a bit hot in your car, Eric -- and love; I couldn't help but get inspired. Of course, I broke all the rules and did the opposite of what any accomplished writer usually does --- I began to read my first-draft to anyone who'd listen.

You're not supposed to be reading your work to others... it's not finished yet! What if you change it? What if you start another project and never finish this one? Well, what if I wasn't aware of all these rules?

Thus, the kids and Eric were my obvious victims. They were an audience of eight ears. Much to my surprise, they loved what I read and wanted to hear more! In retrospect, I believe Eric and the kids were part of a secret conspiracy to make me feel good with what I was putting down on that napkin.

"We can't wait to hear what happens next, Dad," the kids would say with a smile.

"That's pretty good, Doc," Eric would echo.

And since (silly me) I believed them, I was now trapped in a journey of discovery and sharing --- a journey that would ultimately take me back to my own childhood. The child in me hopes you will read **Master and Disciple** with all the wonderment a child possesses. Have a great read!

As always, I welcome your comments and/or your suggestions. Please contact me at:
Jose Luis ("Jay-el") Hinojosa, MD
P.O. Box 530
Johnson, KS 67855
Or go to my exciting website:
www.BooksByDrHinojosa.com

PROLOGUE –

WHO IS THE AUDIENCE FOR THIS BOOK? That's a loaded question because the original title was going to be *How to Stop a Bullet!* However, after much deliberation and feedback from family and friends, I decided to change it to *Master and Disciple*, which is a much more accurate title and does the story justice. Thus, the answer to the original question is: *The audience for this book is both, adults and children.*

This book is intended to teach children, teens, and pre-teens some fundamental, moral, and inspirational lessons about life. Additionally, adults are advised to read this book to their children and *with* their children, thus making it a perfect ice-breaker for initiating dialogue about important topics the child may need to discuss, but is afraid to ask.

Master and Disciple is the story of a father's lessons to his son, and of how the son utilizes these lessons later on in his adult life. It is a wholesome, family story which happens to be told from a martial artist's point of view. The reader will quickly realize that one doesn't have to be a martial artist to learn the valuable lessons contained in *Master and Disciple*.

Notes

Chapter 1

THE WARRIOR

ONCE UPON A TIME, in a small village in South Korea, there was a strong and fearless warrior. He felt more than strong. He felt more than fearless. In fact, he felt invincible!

He had won many battles --- big and small, far and near. He had defeated the best fighters in the land. And rumor had it that he could even stop a bullet!

Those who knew him showered him with gifts and accolades. Those who didn't were awe-stricken with his reputation.

Many important people sought his expertise and teachings. And many more sought his friendship.

However, he hadn't always been strong and fearless. He could recall the days when older, bigger kids picked on him. In fact, he had been the frequent target of the town bully.

Now he was glad he had the skills he had. And, most importantly, he was glad he wasn't such a small, helpless boy anymore.

He was a great man with great skill, and he knew it. Everyone knew it. He was The Man Who Could Stop a Bullet!

He smiled as he reflected on his life. He was happy with all his victories, but he was not satisfied. For, he knew, if he were ever satisfied with his fighting skill he would lose his edge --- the winner's edge.

And when the stakes are high and life and death rest in the balance, every little bit counts. So he wasn't satisfied. He would never be satisfied.

*A FIGHTER WHO IS SATISFIED
WITH HIS SKILL
LOSES THE WINNER'S EDGE.*

The man vividly remembered some specific things about his childhood, especially the times when he was at the losing end of a fight. He noticed that almost everyone who won a fight appeared confident and secure. Pretty much the way his father looked.

Winners were in control. They were not overwhelmed with the chaos surrounding a fight --- the crowd, the screams, and the pain. Oh yes, the pain!

A winner just knew how to take care of business. And winning had become this great warrior's... well, business.

Those deemed worthy of his teachings encountered this as their first lesson:

IN ORDER TO WIN A FIGHT
YOU MUST FIRST
BELIEVE YOU CAN WIN.

"Winning countries," he would say, "believe they can succeed in battle. Winning teachers believe they can transfer their knowledge to their pupils. And even winning parents believe they can raise happy, healthy, and honest children."

The man remembered the time his nose was broken by the town bully and the pain that followed after his father put the nose back to its original position. It was then that he thought, *Maybe if I learn to fight I won't be picked on anymore.*

And so he began to search for a teacher, but not just any teacher. He wanted to learn from the best. He was tired of getting bullied. But most of all, he was tired of hurting all the time.

He searched high and low for a teacher, to no avail. One night, as he sat quietly after dinner, his father asked, "What's wrong, son?"

"I'm tired," he said. "Tired and frustrated."

"With what?"

"I want to learn how to fight and I can't find a teacher."

"I see. It's that bully, right?"

"Right."

"And you think fighting is the answer?"

"I don't know... I just don't want to get beat up anymore."

"I can teach you," said the father.

"You? But you are a healer, not a fighter."

"You are half-right, son," the father answered. He was calm and in control. He was always calm and in control.

"What do you mean?"

"I'll show you," said the father. Then he pulled out a wooden slab with an inscription that read:

HEALING:
THE HIGHEST FORM OF FIGHTING

The boy was confused.

"That's right," the father continued. "All great warriors have trained long and hard to acquire deadly power that may be used during battle. But that same power, when not used for destruction, may be used for construction."

"I don't understand," said the boy.

The father smiled and added, "If we can break someone, then we should also be able to put that someone back together again. Don't you think?"

"I suppose so..."

"Getting into a fight and even hurting someone, while it may require some technical skills, is easy. Healing the ill and the injured... now that's something truly special!"

HURTING & HEALING:
THE TWO FACES OF A FIGHTER'S POWER

"But I need to learn to fight soon," said the boy, "or you're going to have to do more healing... on me!"

"Very well, I will teach you how to fight," said the father. "But first, I will share with you an important story."

"Oh good," said the boy, "I love your stories!"

- • -

ONE DAY A GREAT WARRIOR DECIDED he would like to learn the highest technique in fighting --- the *one technique* that would virtually guarantee victory in combat. He had heard of a very humble master who possessed such a technique. The only problem was that this master was very secretive of his whereabouts. The warrior knew that just finding this elusive master was going to be a monumental challenge in and of itself.

And just as he suspected, he quickly ran into one dead end after another. Pretty soon the entire town heard of this warrior's quest and of his mounting dilemma. And since everyone regarded him highly, the people decided to unite and help him find the master who could not be found.

Weeks and even months went by until... on a beautiful spring day; the great warrior met the once-elusive master, who was busy working on his garden.

"I wish to learn the ultimate technique," said the warrior.

"Did you say *ultimate* technique?" asked the master.

"Yes. I am a great warrior now but I cannot be fulfilled until I learn the highest level of fighting... and this is what you must teach me."

"Very well," said the master. Then he pointed his right index finger to the sky and said, "Can you find a bird atop one of those two trees?"

The warrior quickly and easily spotted a bird on each of the two majestic trees in the master's backyard. "I do," he said.

"When you bring one of those two birds down to the ground I will teach you."

No sooner had the master said this that the warrior took out a small knife and threw it with such speed and accuracy toward the closest tree... bringing down one of the birds to its demise.

"There!" exclaimed the warrior. "Is that what you wanted?"

The master shook his head and closed his eyes softly. Then, after a moment of concentration, he let out a yell so powerful that the trees shook. Even the great warrior was thrown off balance for a moment. The second bird fell to the ground at the feet of the warrior, who was still trying to regain his balance.

"Wow! That *is* a great technique!" he yelled. "Show me how to do that!"

"I could show you," said the master, "but you said you wanted to learn the *ultimate* technique."

"Well, what can be better than that?" asked the warrior. "You killed that bird without even touching it!"

The master closed his eyes once again, and just as he did before, he concentrated for a moment. Then he yelled another thunderous time and the bird opened its eyes, stood up, and flew away. "Healing," said the master, "is the ultimate technique."

- • -

"WOW!" SAID THE BOY. "And did the master teach the warrior how to do that?"

"Not immediately," said the father. "The master did take the warrior on as his student, though. And the warrior practiced his *ultimate* technique for many years until he began to develop the art of healing."

"Maybe you should teach me the ultimate technique first," said the boy.

"No, son," said the father, "first I will teach you how to defend yourself physically. You will learn how to fight."

"But I've never seen you fight." The boy was skeptical. "Are you sure you know how to fight?"

"It is true you've never seen me fight --- and I hope you never do."

"Huh?"

"The fact that you've never *seen* me fight doesn't mean I don't know how."

"There you go again, father. I honestly don't know what you're trying to tell me."

"Let me explain," said the father. "Have you ever heard of the art of fighting without fighting?"

"Fighting without fighting? You're kidding, right?"

"No. I'm very serious, son. When I was around your age I realized I didn't like to fight."

"Why not?"

"Because there were other things I enjoyed."

"Like taking care of people?"

"That's right. I always knew I wanted to be a healer. And so I learned to fight with such skill and determination that pretty soon I didn't have to get into any more fights."

"Because everyone was afraid of you?"

"No, not everyone... but enough to leave me alone, which gave me more time to pursue other interests."

"So when you were studying healing you didn't get into many fights?"

"Correct," said the father. "And I quickly learned that the reason I wasn't getting picked on was because I stood up for myself."

"You mean, you stood up and you fought?"

"No. More than a physical battle," explained the father, "fighting is in the *mind* and in the *heart*."

"And just how is my mind or my heart going to defeat the bully?"

"In order to win a fight," said the father, "you must first believe you can win."

"But he's much bigger and much stronger than I."

"Do you or don't you wish to defend yourself and defeat this bully?"

"Yes sir. I want to win."

"Then you must believe this to be true... in your mind and in your heart."

The boy was mesmerized. He was learning from the best teacher --- his father, the healer.

"Remember son, if you believe he will defeat you, then he probably will. However, if you believe you will win, then you stand a good chance of winning."

"So that's it?" said the boy. "I just have to believe and I'll win?"

"No. First you believe, then you train hard --- *then* you can win."

And so the young boy started to train diligently. He would quickly find that believing in himself was more difficult than he imagined. How could he --- how could anyone --- believe in someone who kept getting beat up? Being the victim surely didn't instill any confidence in him. He was now ready to change all that.

He compensated for his lack of confidence and low self-esteem by doing more than was asked of him. When his father wanted him to practice a certain kick or a certain punch fifty times, he would do it one hundred times. If he were told to run for ten minutes, he would run for thirty. And as his physical abilities grew, so did his confidence and self-esteem.

One day the unthinkable happened: he stood up against the bully! No, he didn't win the fight; he won something much greater --- the bully's respect. And much to his surprise, that would be the last time the bully ever picked on him.

And so he began to understand the art of fighting without fighting --- and the fact that fights can actually be won or lost without anyone ever throwing a single punch. The young boy smiled because he knew his father was right all along. He had learned his first valuable lesson in fighting and in life:

IF YOU THINK YOU CAN, YOU CAN.
IF YOU THINK YOU CAN'T, YOU CAN'T.
EITHER WAY, YOU'RE PROBABLY RIGHT.

Chapter 2

LOOK FIRST

THE GREAT WARRIOR ENJOYED THINKING about his early days as a young warrior student. Almost reflexively, he touched the bridge of his nose --- just one of the many injuries he had sustained in his illustrious career. And just like they did back when his nose had been broken, his eyes welled-up. Today, a tear would find its way down his face.

He saw himself as a boy, hearing his father's words:

BEFORE YOU FIGHT,
YOU MUST FIRST LOOK
AT YOUR OPPONENT.

"Well of course," said the eager disciple. "You have to *see* who you're fighting, right?"

"Not necessarily. I have fought in total darkness."

"*Total* darkness?"

"That's right. Sometimes, even the moon will fail to show up during battle. So you have to rely on all your senses. Now, you tell me the five senses that everyone is familiar with and I'll tell you about the sixth sense."

"There's a sixth sense?"

"Yes. And it's very real."

"What is it?"

"Nah-ah," the father said as he shook his head. "You first."

"Very well. Let's see... there's sight, smell, taste, hearing, and touch. Did I miss any?"

"Yes, the sixth sense."

"That's not fair. How can I be expected to know something I haven't been taught yet?"

"Very good thinking, son. You've earned this one." The father paused for a second before continuing. "The sixth sense is an inner voice, a gut feeling. It's your conscience. It's the wisdom and energy of everyone in our family who came before us."

"Do I have *your* wisdom and energy inside me?"

The father smiled and said, "Yes you do, son. And it's part of your sixth sense."

"Does everyone have a sixth sense?"

"Everyone has it, but some people learn to nurture and to develop it, just like you're learning to nurture and develop your fighting skills."

"Good!" The boy's wheels turned inside his head as he thought for a moment. Then he said, "I want to learn to fight at night, just like you."

"That's fine," said the father, "but it's preferable to *actually see* your opponent --- especially to see into his eyes."

"Why is that?" asked the boy.

Then the father said something that would forever be engrained in the boy's mind:

THE EYES ARE THE WINDOWS
TO THE SOUL.

"What does that mean?" asked the boy.

"It means that you can learn a lot by looking into someone's eyes."

"How so?"

"Well, you can see if he's focused and concentrated, or nervous and scared. You can see if he means what he says or if he's just bluffing. You can even see if he's about to attack or about to faint."

"What if I see in my opponent's eyes that he's about to tear me to shreds?"

"Then you might be in trouble... and that's also why part of your training is running."

"You mean... lose face and run away?"

"What I'm telling you will *save* your face, son. And yes, run as fast and as far as your legs will take you."

"But won't all the other kids make fun of me?"

"So let them say as they please. Remember, words don't have to hurt, but kicks and punches do. "

"Oh, you don't know, father..."

"What don't I know?"

"That kids my age can say some vicious things these days."

"Whatever is said in the negative can be easily turned into something positive."

"What do you mean?"

"Usually, when someone says something bad about somebody else, they're really showing their insecurities and weaknesses. So I want you to remember this..."

STICKS & STONES MAY BREAK MY BONES
BUT WORDS WILL NEVER HURT ME ---

IF I USE WORDS
AS TOOLS FOR CONSTRUCTION,
NOT WEAPONS OF DESTRUCTION.

As he uttered these words, the warrior remembered a story when he was a child about a legendary man. A man of few words and great actions. A gentle man whose name was as much a mystery as the feat for which he gained notoriety. He was simply known as The Man Who Could Stop an Arrow.

- • -

THIS MAN, SO GOES THE LEGEND, was not a fighter in the true sense of the word. However, he was so fast and so agile that one night, as he walked back into town, he was attacked by three armed men. Because he offered no resistance, he should have been let go after they took his money. In a more perfect world, that would have been the case. But those were violent times --- times wrought with social and political unrest.

And so, the robbers had other plans. One of them shot an arrow into the man's chest. The man dropped to the ground, clutching his chest. When the attackers walked up to the fallen man they saw something they would never forget. The man's clenched right hand opened to reveal the arrow's point, just before it reached his chest!

The man's eyes then pierced those of his attackers like daggers. The three, in turn, ran in horror as if they had just seen a ghost.

Nobody really found out who this mysterious man was. His legend was born just the same. And curiously enough, there was much less violence in that town after that night.

- • -

AS A BOY, THE WARRIOR HAD ALWAYS been intrigued by this story. He wondered if he would ever meet The Man Who Could Stop an Arrow. He wanted to learn how to stop an arrow too.

One day in the backyard, as his father taught him defenses against a stick, he asked if his father believed the story.

"Of course I do," said the father.

"Why do you sound so sure? Don't you think maybe it's just a legend and somebody made it all up?"

The father smiled and said, "Come son. Come closer and tell me what you see."

He showed the boy his hands. The palm of his right hand was badly scarred.

"It's you! You're The Man Who Could Stop an Arrow!"

"That's right, son."

"Why didn't you tell me before?"

"Because it wouldn't have made any difference."

"What do you mean?"

"I mean that I was *still* going to teach you everything I knew."

"Even how to stop an arrow?"

The father laughed. "That, my son, was pure luck."

"Luck? I don't think it was luck. *Nobody* thinks it was luck."

The father thought for a moment. Then he said, "Luck doesn't just come to you. You have to be prepared for it."

"But how do you *prepare* to find luck?"

The father held up a stick and said, "Watch closely, son. I'm about to give you the secret formula for finding all the good luck in the world. Are you ready?"

"Of course, of course!"

Then the father used the stick to write the following formula on the ground:

$$PREPARATION$$
$$+$$
$$OPPORTUNITY$$
$$+$$
$$ACTION$$
$$=$$
$$LUCK$$

And from that day on, the boy considered himself the luckiest person in the world.

Chapter 3

THE 80-20 RULE

"FATHER, FATHER!" SAID THE BOY. "It's been exactly two weeks since the bully picked on me. I'm just so lucky!"

The boy's father smiled and said, "Excellent, son. Do you think you're ready for another lesson?"

"Oh, yes! I can't wait... honestly."

"Very well. Have I told you about the eighty-twenty rule?"

"No sir, you have not."

"Those are two important numbers you should remember. Eighty and twenty. They total, of course, one hundred percent."

"Am I going to have to do mathematics when I'm defending myself?"

The father laughed. "Not exactly, son. Eighty-twenty applies to a lot of principles both, in life and in fighting."

"For instance?"

"For instance..." the father then stopped himself. "Let me ask you," he finally said, "what is your strongest stance?"

"Well, the front stance, of course."

"That's right. And why is it so strong?"

"Because most of my weight is in my... front leg?" The boy thought that perhaps this was a trick question.

"Correct," said the father. "About eighty-percent of your weight is in your front leg when you're in a front stance. You are on more solid ground that way and you can deliver a more powerful technique from the front stance."

The boy assumed a front stance as his father continued explaining.

"That is definitely a stance you want to be in," said the father, "if you wish to have power in your attacks."

"So *that's* what you mean when you talk about the eighty-twenty rule!"

"That's right, that and more."

"There's more?"

"Don't worry," the father laughed again, "just keep those numbers in mind and you'll do fine."

"Okay, I can remember eighty-twenty makes the front stance strong. What else should I know?"

"Eighty percent of your wins are produced by about twenty percent of your techniques."

"No, that can't be true... can it?"

"Sure it can. Take this, for instance. Which would you rather do, one kick one thousand times or one thousand kicks one time each? Remember, either way you're doing one thousand kicks, so you can't say *neither*."

"I would take... the one kick."

"Why?"

"Because I only have to remember one kick."

"That's right! And also, you would have learned that one technique so well that you may not need many other techniques to defend yourself."

"Wow!"

"Remind me to tell you the story about the fox and the cat."

"The fox and the cat? What does that have to do with this?"

"I'll tell you in a moment, but first let me finish going over the eighty-twenty rule."

"Alright, go ahead."

"If you can learn and retain eighty percent of what I teach you..."

"Yes, yes?" the boy was eager to hear more.

"Well, then you don't really need the other twenty percent, now do you?"

Both laughed out loud. It was a great father-son moment --- and a great learning environment for both.

- • -

THE GREAT WARRIOR WAS STARTLED by a knock on the door. It was one of his disciples, the son of the Emperor. The door was open, but the young man did not enter. He stood at the doorway and said, "Excuse me, sir. I know I wasn't scheduled for a lesson today, but I felt I needed to see you."

"Come in, come in," said the warrior.

"Thank you, sir."

"What is it that you needed to see me about?"

"I just wanted to get away from the house."

"Oh? What happened?"

"It's my little brother. I was trying to practice what you taught me yesterday..."

"And?"

"And he just kept talking and talking. He wouldn't stop."

"Well, that's no reason to leave... unless you're not telling me everything."

"I lost my temper. I got angry and yelled at him. I yelled and yelled, and I couldn't control myself. I was very angry... so I left so I wouldn't hit him."

"You would have hit your own little brother for something like that?"

"Yes sir."

"Listen to me... when a fighter loses control, then he cannot win."

"But if I have trained hard. I can win, right?"

"Training only gives you an advantage over someone who is not trained or who has received little training. It does not guarantee victory."

"It doesn't? I thought if I trained hard I would have many wins."

"You can have many wins, but training isn't everything. Have I told you about the eighty-twenty rule?"

"No. I don't believe you have."

"Eighty percent of your wins will come before a single punch is ever thrown. Therefore, it is imperative that you are in control --- for a person who cannot control himself cannot control another person."

Then the warrior said something that would change the way the young man looked at life:

BEFORE YOU CAN CONQUER OTHERS
YOU MUST FIRST CONQUER YOURSELF.

"If you can control your emotions and your movements," the great warrior continued, "then with your training and skills you should be able to emerge victorious about eighty percent of the time without ever having to fight."

"Wow! I think I understand what you're trying to tell me." The young man continued, "You're right, when I was angry and yelling I don't think I even knew who I was, much less know what to do in battle."

"I'm glad you realize that."

"I'll try harder to control my anger."

"Good. You do that and you'll be on your way to *truly* knowing yourself and to becoming enlightened."

"Whoa... please slow down a bit. I didn't understand a word of what you just said."

"What part didn't you understand?"

"Me? Enlightened? How can that ever happen? I thought that was reserved for great warriors like you."

The warrior smiled as he said, "Let me show you the way to enlightenment. Follow me." He led the young man to the backyard, where the warrior's father had taught him many lessons. He then picked up a stick and wrote the following on the ground:

TO KNOW HOW TO FIGHT IS TO HAVE KNOWLEDGE,
TO KNOW OTHERS IS TO HAVE WISDOM,
BUT TO KNOW YOURSELF IS TO BE ENLIGHTENED.

"That is beautiful," said the young man, "but I'm only a beginner. I'm just learning how to fight." He bowed his head and started to leave, but the great warrior stopped him.

"Wait!" The warrior walked over to the young man and put a hand on his shoulder. "Everyone has to go through the same steps. There are no short cuts. So, do you want to *tell* me what you were trying to practice when your little brother interrupted you?"

The young man felt better and said, "Sure! I have been practicing three, no... four more different ways of taking down an opponent." He started to pace anxiously. He wanted to show his teacher what he could do.

"Four?" said the warrior. "You mean, four besides the one I taught you?"

"Yes, sir."

The great warrior remembered a lesson his father had taught him once when he was as eager as his disciple was now.

"Sit down, please," he said. "Let me tell you the story of the fox and the cat."

"The fox and the cat? I don't think I want to hear about some animals right now," said the young man. "What I really want to do is show you what I have been practicing."

"You can show me later," said the warrior, "but right now you will sit quietly and listen."

- • -

"ONCE UPON A TIME," SAID THE FATHER, "there was a very sly fox. This fox was not only interested in surviving a hunt, but also in looking good in the process. He was very good, but also very vain."

"And what about the cat?" said the boy warrior.

"Well, one day the fox walked up to a small, timid cat and made fun of him."

"Why did he do that?

"Because the fox was mean   and because he knew that the cat didn't know very much about defending himself nor about getting out of harm's way. In fact, the cat was only good at one thing and one thing only... climbing trees."

"But I bet he also knew how to land, right? *All* cats know how to land."

"You're right, son --- cats will always land on their feet. So you can see, the cat's skills were limited, but he knew what he knew and he was good at it. And the fox laughed and laughed at the poor little cat because the fox had many skills. He could run, he could jump, he could hide, and he could do a host of other things whenever he was attacked. So he had many ways of escaping and saving himself, and the cat didn't."

"So what happened?"

"One day, a bear appeared while the fox was busy talking and picking on the cat. The bear attacked them both. He didn't care whom he captured. He was hungry."

"Did the cat run up a tree?"

"Yes, he did. In fact, he did the only thing he was any good at."

"And the fox?"

"Well, the fox took a few seconds to decide what escape tactic he was going to use. Needless to say, by the time he decided what to do, the bear was already upon him. The fox became that night's dinner and the cat... well; the cat witnessed everything from atop the tree. And he was glad he was good at something, even if it was something as simple as climbing a tree."

- • -

"I GUESS," SAID THE YOUNG MAN, "you want me to continue practicing the one technique you showed me, right?"

"That's right," said the warrior, "at least for one year. Then maybe you'll be ready for more."

And so the young man went back to his home having learned two important elements of battle:
>1) You cannot expect to control others if you cannot control yourself, and
>2) You must practice one technique over and over until it is absolutely mastered before trying to learn something new.

Notes

_____
_____
_____
_____
_____
_____
_____
_____
_____
_____
_____
_____
_____
_____
_____
_____
_____
_____
_____

Chapter 4

THE EMPEROR

"HOW LONG HAS HE BEEN IN BED?" asked the warrior. He had been summoned to the home of the Emperor because the Emperor's eldest son, the warrior's student, was ill.   "The Sun has come and gone thrice," said the Emperor. "He has not opened his eyes, and the fire inside of him is angry. Even with all the power I command, I find myself helpless."

"Has the town healer seen him already?"

"Yes... and he says he cannot help him. Can *you* do anything for my son? Please, I beg you. He thinks very highly of you, as do all of us."

The great warrior stood beside the bed, put his hands together, and concentrated on them. He breathed deeply, in through his nose and out through his mouth, a few times. He then rubbed his hands together very vigorously until what looked like a glow appeared around them.

The Emperor and his assistants could not believe what they were witnessing.

"Please," said the warrior, "everyone stand back."

They did as they were told, all the while in awe of this man.

He placed his left hand over his student's eyes and his right hand a few inches below the student's navel. Then he closed his eyes and resumed his slow, focused breathing. After a few minutes, which seemed like an eternity to the Emperor, he took as long a breath as he could then let out a thundering yell not unlike those he used in battle. The room seemed to tremble --- and a few of the witnesses screamed with surprise.

The warrior had finished. He removed his hands and then stood, as if waiting for something to happen.

His student's eyes slowly opened! Everyone in the room rejoiced and began to clap.

The warrior raised his arms to quiet everyone down and said, "Our Emperor's son, my student, is not well yet, but he will be. Right now he needs silence... and some water."

The Emperor motioned for water, then asked, "How did you do that? I thought your skills were only in fighting!"

"The highest form of fighting is healing, your Excellency."

"But how did you learn to do that?"

The warrior smiled and said, "I had the best teacher." He looked back at his student, who by now was being helped to some water. Then he turned to the Emperor and said, "Your Excellency, fighting and healing are one and the same."

"Oh? And just how can you explain that?"

"Let me tell you about the time when my father taught me both the healing touch and fighting skills all in one lesson."

"Really?" The Emperor was intrigued. "Continue."

"One evening, before my training session and as I reviewed some stick attacks, I severely injured my right shoulder..."

- • -

"OUCH!" YELLED THE YOUNG WARRIOR.

"What's the matter?" asked the father as he arrived to his son's training session.

"I can't move my arm... and it really, really hurts!"

"Relax and slow down your breathing, son. You are breathing too fast."

The young warrior did his best to avoid a state of hyperventilation, but he was having difficulty.

"You already have one injury. We do not want to have to tend to another problem if you continue breathing so fast that you pass out, do we?"

"But I don't think I can tolerate much more of this... this pain. Ouch!"

The father moved effortlessly and with great speed. He transformed into the great healer that he was. He brought his hands together and focused his eyes on them. As he concentrated on his breathing, he began to rub his hands. He rubbed and rubbed and his eyes never wandered. He seemed not to even blink.

Then the boy warrior saw it --- a beautiful glow enveloped his father's hands.

"Wow! What's happening?" asked the boy.

But the father did not answer, for he had become a *focus* of energy --- a source of infinite power.

Then, without saying a word, the father placed one hand on the injured shoulder and the other just below the navel --- a point which, the boy had been taught, was the origin of all energy.

The father's eyes closed again and he resumed slow, concentrated breathing. All the while, the glow on the boy's shoulder and abdomen seemed to intensify. Then, without warning, the father let out an earth-shattering yell. A nearby tree branch broke and the father opened his eyes.

"I don't feel anything," said the boy. "It doesn't hurt anymore!" He moved his shoulder back and forth and checked it for any pain. He found none. "Teach me to do that, please?"

The father prepared a sling for his son's arm and said, "In due time. But first, I want you to wear this for five days and five nights. Oh, and you will not be able to practice for a total of ten days and ten nights."

"Ten! Why? I feel better already!"

"You need the time to heal properly. But that's okay; you could use the rest anyway."

"How do you know I need rest?"

"There are some things that a father just knows... but tell me, son, how did this happen?"

"It was this stick! It doesn't want to do what I tell it. It's misbehaving."

"Weapons do not behave --- they are *behaved upon*," said the father.

BEHIND EVERY WEAPON IS A PERSON.

"Let me show you something." The father placed a knife on the ground and said, "Watch this knife. Do you see it move?"

"No."

"Do you see it misbehave, perhaps?"

"No --- it's just sitting there."

"Precisely!" said the father. "By itself, a weapon is nothing. It can harm no one. But it comes to life once a person picks it up. See?"

He picked up the knife and began to slice and stab through the air with a grace and beauty that the boy had only previously seen in dances, not in fighting.

"Wow! It looks like you're dancing."

"Thank you. I do love to dance," said the father as he continued his demonstration.

"Is that the way a knife is used... like a dance?"

The father finished the knife routine and said, "Yes, like a dance with a partner. And in this case, the knife is my partner."

"How can the knife be your partner?"

"Let me explain something," said the father as he put his arm around his son's shoulder. "In order for a dance to provide enjoyment, it requires two people moving as one. Otherwise, somebody's toes are going to be hurting."

The boy laughed.

"The same," he added, "applies to any weapon. In order for you to succeed in weaponry, you and your weapon must move as one."

BE ONE WITH YOUR WEAPON.

The young warrior looked at his weapon, the stick, and then grabbed his shoulder. It felt much better. He knew that in ten days he would have a much different appreciation of weapons. He couldn't wait to learn to use his weapon as an extension of himself. His weapon would become a part of his anatomy. The young warrior and his weapon would be one and the same.

Notes

Chapter 5

THE BEST FIGHTER

"FATHER!" SAID THE BOY. "When I grow up I want to be the best fighter in the land."

"Good for you, son. That is a most remarkable goal."

"How long do you think it will take if I train three to four hours each day?"

"Three to four hours?" The father then made some calculations in his head. "Three to four hours translates into approximately... ten years."

"Wow! That's a long time." Being young in thinking and eager in spirit, the boy then said, "And if I train six hours each day?"

Once again the father calculated in his head. "Six hours per day translates into approximately... fifteen years."

"Fifteen! I don't get it. Shouldn't it take less time if I train more each day?"

Then the father said something the boy would never forget:

ONLY ONE EYE CAN FOCUS
ON THE WAY
WHEN THE OTHER IS ASTRAY.

"Sometimes," said the father, "if you relax and try not to think so much about your destination, then your journey will be much more enjoyable."

"But I am still enjoying my training. I love fighting and I believe that if I train hard enough I will become the best fighter soon!"

"That is not always the case, son. In fact, it may actually take longer to achieve your goals when you are not giving your best."

"But I am!" The boy was exasperated. "I am trying very hard to become the best."

"You may be trying too hard."

"What? First you say I'm not giving my best... then you say I'm trying too hard!" The boy was more confused than ever. "Can you please make up your mind?"

The father laughed as he sometimes did when his son, the young warrior, challenged his teachings. "If fighting is the only thing you do, then you cannot be the best fighter you can be. However, if you develop other talents and skills you can bring their energy and experiences to your fighting. This, my son, will make you a much better fighter."

"I see," said the boy. "I think I will train two hours each day... but what else should I do the rest of the day?"

"There are many things. You can study dance --- your body will learn new ways of movement that can only help a warrior."

"I'll study dance, then."

"You can also study art or music --- they heighten your artistic awareness."

"That's true. I will also study art and music."

"You can learn another language --- the more people that you can communicate with, the less misunderstandings and fewer fights you will be involved in."

"Wow! It seems that I should also learn another language, right?"

The father smiled and said, "Son, there is an entire life of learning. You do not have to learn everything in one day. Take your time and enjoy yourself, but always remember that whatever else you learn will make you a better fighter because a more complete person is also a more complete fighter."

"Okay, I will train two hours each day and I choose dance as my other activity for now. Will you teach me?"

"Yes, son," said the father. "But you must still do your best."

"Well, I will be doing my best because I will also be learning dance. You said that if I learn something else I will be a better fighter."

"Correct, I said that. But the *effort* you give to your actions must be your best effort. Otherwise, you will not be happy with yourself and you will punish yourself for not trying hard enough."

The boy thought for a while then said, "How about when I am ill? I may not be able to give my best effort then. What will I do?"

"That's an excellent question, son, and it tells me that you are serious about improving yourself and being the best you can be."

"So, is it possible to do my best when I am ill?"

"Yes," said the father.

The boy was dumbfounded. He thought he heard wrong, so he reiterated, "So, I *can* do my best when I am ill?"

"That is correct because your best will change from day to day and from situation to situation. Of course, when you are ill your best cannot be the same as when you are strong and healthy. The one thing you will realize is if you do not do your best, regardless of your condition, you will know it in your heart and in your mind."

"How will I know?"

"You will know it because you will experience anger, self-pity, and frustration. When that occurs, you did not do your best. On the other hand, when you did your best, you will more than likely feel happiness, fulfillment, and contentment... regardless of the outcome."

"You mean, I could do my best and still lose a fight?

"Yes."

"And I would feel happy about that?"

"You would be at peace with yourself knowing that you did the best that you could at that moment. Not too many people feel especially proud of losing a fight, but they should be able to accept that and move forward. There is always something new to learn that may help you for next time."

"I get it!" said the boy. "If I am a happier person because I am healthy and I am learning, then I will also be a better fighter."

"And... a better son," said the father. He was proud his son was on the right path toward a happy and fulfilling life.

*IN ANY TEST
ALWAYS DO YOUR BEST.*

"Sit down," said the father. "I want to share with you a story of what can happen when you always do your best."

– • –

A YOUNG BOY WISHED TO LEARN how to defend himself against his neighbors, who were bullying him on a daily basis. He knocked on the door of a great teacher, but he soon found out that the teacher was now retired and he could not help him. The boy pleaded with the teacher, to no avail. He pleaded and pleaded, and even begged... and went as far as to say he'd do anything as long as the teacher would come out of retirement to teach one last time.

The old man, touched by the boy's perseverance, finally said he'd teach him if and only if the boy could uproot a small tree that stood in the front yard. The tree was partially blocking the view from within the house, and the old man needed it removed.

Every day, the boy came to the old man's house to try and uproot the small tree. He was unsuccessful. As the weeks and the months passed, word spread of the boy's efforts. In fact, the young boy gave his best effort each and every day. Even when he was ill, the boy showed up and tried to uproot the tree. Of course, his effort was not the same as when he was healthy, but nevertheless he tried his best.

As the boy grew to his teens and then into adulthood, the tree became a handsome and imposing figure in the front yard. Early one winter morning, a persistent knocking was heard at the old man's front door. By now, the old man walked a bit slower, so it took him a while to get to the door and open it.

When he opened the door he saw the boy, now a fully-grown and very muscular man, breathing heavily. Behind him lay the great tree --- it had been uprooted!

The strong man managed to ask in between breaths when his lessons would start, to which the old man replied, "You do not need any more lessons. No one in their right mind will ever want to fight a strong man like you --- somebody who never gives up and who always gives his best effort."

- • -

"HE ALWAYS GAVE HIS BEST, he never quit, and..." said the boy warrior, "he won without ever having to fight!"

"Son," said the proud father, "I do believe you are learning your lessons quite well."

The boy laughed and said, "Well of course! It's always easier when you're learning from the best."

Notes

Chapter 6

CHOICES

THE YOUNG WARRIOR GOT HOME from school with a smile on his face. "Today I beat up a boy in my class," he said with great pride.

"What? What happened?" asked the father.

"A boy was looking at my work, so I punched him on the nose." The young warrior was proud of himself. "And you know... he didn't even see it coming!"

"Why would you do something like that?"

"Well... because he was doing something wrong. Our teacher told us we're not supposed to copy someone else's work."

"No, you are not," said the father. "But that is no reason to get into a fight, now is it?"

"But what he did was wrong."

"True... and what *you* did was also wrong. I hope I am not teaching you how to fight so you can just fight any time you want to. That is really an abuse of your skills and a misuse of my teachings."

"So, I guess I shouldn't have hit him, huh?" The boy was starting to feel guilty and ashamed.

"Son, you must..."

CHOOSE YOUR BATTLES WISELY.

"What does that mean?"

"It means that you decide which battles are worth fighting. And keep in mind that the battles you choose define what is truly important in your life."

"I don't understand."

"Sit down so I can explain," said the father. "Each and every day there will be things that others say or do that you may not agree with. Your idea of a *perfect* world may not be somebody else's idea of a perfect world."

The boy listened intently.

"Imagine what kind of life we would lead if we got into a fight every time something did not go our way. We would spend a lot of time and energy in small, meaningless fights. And that, my son, is a total misuse of talent, skills, and effort."

"Wow, I don't want to be in fights all the time."

The father walked over to the boy and looked into his eyes. "Son," he said, "pretty soon our entire life would be a series of little battles. All our energy would be spent on relatively unimportant things, and when we truly need to go into battle we may not be ready nor in the best possible condition."

"I get it," said the boy. "I should not fight for the sake of fighting, right?"

"That is correct," said the father. "One should fight for what is truly important --- love, life, and honor."

"You are so right," said the boy. "If I constantly get into fights I may be so busy with little stuff that I may not know when the big one is in front of me."

THE BATTLES WE CHOOSE DEFINE
WHAT IS TRULY IMPORTANT TO US.

"Very good, son. I see you are getting the message." He laughed at his son's choice of words. "Remember, the *big one,* as you call it, is really three things: love, life, and honor."

"Yes, sir. I'll remember that."

"A smart warrior does not risk his life over little, insignificant things or possessions. Material things can be replaced... but a life can never return."   "I hadn't thought about it that way, father. I guess I should be more careful."

The father nodded. "Think about this, son. When a person dies, what does he take with him?"

"What do you mean what does he take?"

"What *can* a person take when he is dead?"

"Nothing, I think."

"Nothing is right. When we die, we cannot take our money and we cannot take our possessions. So you better be sure that the fight you are involved in is worth fighting."

"Can we take our memories?"

"Well, maybe that we can take. But on the other hand, if you survive battle there is always another day to replace those material things that you may have lost while you were busy defending the big one."

"Love, life, and honor," said the boy. "See, I remembered."

"Very good, son. Very good."

- • -

"CHOOSE YOUR BATTLES WISELY," said the great warrior.

"You mean," said the disciple, "I can choose when to fight?"

"Yes, you *should* choose when to fight and when not to fight. That way you shall win every fight."

"But how will I know when it's time to fight?"

"Trust me," said the warrior, "you will know. Have I told you the story of the carver and the old man?"

"No sir, you have not."

"Sit down then, and listen..."

- • -

AN OLD, FRAGILE-LOOKING MAN came into town one day and asked for the best artisan around, for he needed a carving made. He was directed to a highly-skilled carver who also happened to be quite strong physically. When the old man arrived at the shop, the carver immediately recognized him.

"Aren't you a famous martial artist?" he asked.

"I don't know about *famous*, but I have practiced the martial arts for many years," the old man replied.

"You look so old and so frail!" he said. "It must be very sad to be old."

"Yes," said the old man, "it is very sad... but I believe it is far sadder to never have reached old age."

The carver snapped back, "Are you threatening me, old man?"

The old man remained calm and said, "We all go through the same stages in life. One day, you too will be old and weak like I am."

The carver had heard enough. "Well, I am not old and I am not weak! I have won many fights and I bet I can defeat you right now!"

"I do not wish to fight."

"Oh, but I do... and besides, I've always wanted to defeat a great martial arts master like yourself."

And as soon as he said this he attacked the old man. He leapt into the air... but just as quickly, the old man let out a yell so powerful that the carver's attack was suddenly stopped in mid-flight. The carver fell backwards almost as if a force more powerful than he had taken him down. He could swear the thunderous sound came from the depths of the earth. He just lay there in shock, looking at the old man's eyes.

The carver got up slowly and hesitated for a moment before initiating a second attack. This time the old man's concentrated look froze the young, strong artisan in his tracks. He could not move! It was as if his feet were rooted on the ground and he was stuck there.

The young, strong carver finally conceded defeat and asked the old man, "How did you defeat me? You are old and weak... and I am young and strong."

"It's very simple," said the old man. "You were only interested in defeating a weak, old man.   But I...   I was ready to die during battle."

HE WHO IS WILLING TO DIE DURING BATTLE
IS THE MOST DANGEROUS OPPONENT.

"You were ready to die?" asked the carver.

"Yes. I have already lived a long and fruitful life. I have nothing else to do; nothing else to prove. I have seen my children grow up and become happy and productive members of society. I am ready to die, thus I am not hindered in any way. Are *you* ready to die?"

"Of course not!" said the carver. "I still have a lot of things I would like to do in my life."

"That is why you should not fight just to prove you are strong. Everybody probably already knows that. You must choose your battles wisely."

- • -

"WOW!" SAID THE DISCIPLE. "That is a wonderful story. And what happened to the carver?"

"I'm glad you asked," said the great warrior. "After much insisting, the old man took him as an apprentice."

"Hey, wait a minute! Didn't the old man say that he had already lived a full life and had nothing more to do?"

The warrior smiled. "That is right."

"So why would he teach somebody who wanted to kill him?"

"Because the old man had come to that town *specifically* to teach the young carver his art."

"Wait a minute... what's going on?"

The warrior laughed out loud and said, "The old man had heard of a strong artisan who was a great fighter, but who also needed some guidance. So he came to find him."

"Oh, I get it," said the disciple. "He didn't *need* any carvings at all!"

"I see you were paying attention," said the great warrior. "And I'm glad." He thought for a moment and then added, "I may need some work done... are you any good at wood carving?" They both laughed.

Chapter 7

ALWAYS BE READY

THE BOY WAS GLAD he told his father of the school incident. He learned a valuable lesson because of it. And since his excitement was too large too late in the evening, he had a difficult time falling asleep that night. He tossed and turned, finally getting up and out of bed. He was not sure what to do, so he walked over to his father's room.

As the father lay in bed the boy approached him. He was shocked to notice one of his father's eyes wide open, seemingly looking at something. Perhaps, looking at him!

"Son!" he said, getting up. "What are you doing?"

"Ahhh!" the boy yelled. "Your eye!" He continued, "Your eye... was looking right at me."

The father laughed. "Well of course, son. I always sleep with one eye open."

"What for?"

"So I will not be caught off guard."

"But who would want to fight somebody who is asleep?"

"Many fighters, son... especially the smart ones."

"I don't get it."

"One of the basic principles of winning in fighting is..."

ATTACK WHEN YOUR OPPONENT
IS NOT READY FOR YOU.

The father continued, "That is why many warriors have been attacked in their sleep. Because most people are not ready for battle during sleep."

"But you *saw* me, didn't you? When I entered your room?"

"Yes, son. I did."

"So that means that *you* were ready for battle, right?"

"That is right. I was ready for battle and I was ready for peace. I was even ready for my own son to sneak up on me."

"Sorry about that. I didn't mean to."

"That is alright, son," said the father. "With the help of a special prayer, the *Warrior's Prayer*, one can pretty much be ready for anything... at any time of the day or night."

"The *Warrior's Prayer*?" The boy thought for a moment then added, "I didn't think warriors needed to pray."

"Oh yes, everyone needs to pray. And warriors are no exception. They risk their lives every day. And besides, a little extra help never hurt anyone, right?"

"Right, father."

"Would you like to learn it?"

"Oh, yes," said the boy. "I want to learn as much as I can."

"Very well then." The father took a slow, deep breath and recited...

AS I LAY ME DOWN TO SLEEP,
ONE EYE OPEN I SHALL KEEP.
IF I'M WEAK I MAY DO WRONG,
MAKE ME PURE, WISE, AND STRONG.

"That's a great prayer!" said the boy. "Did you make that up?"

"No, son, I did not. This prayer has been passed down for many generations. It is part of a warrior's belief system."

"Do all warriors believe in prayer?"

"Not all, but the ones who do are more at peace with themselves. I, myself, always feel better when I pray."

"I'll start praying every night too," said the boy.

"Good for you, son. Just think of this as a special request for protection from the God of War."

"Okay, I'll do that. I guess I could use the protection."

"We can all use it," said the father. "We can all use it."

That night the boy went back to bed after reciting the newly learned *Warrior's Prayer*. He tried his best to keep one eye open.

He could not.

He was still young.

Notes

_____

_____

_____

_____

_____

_____

_____

_____

_____

_____

_____

_____

_____

_____

_____

_____

_____

_____

_____

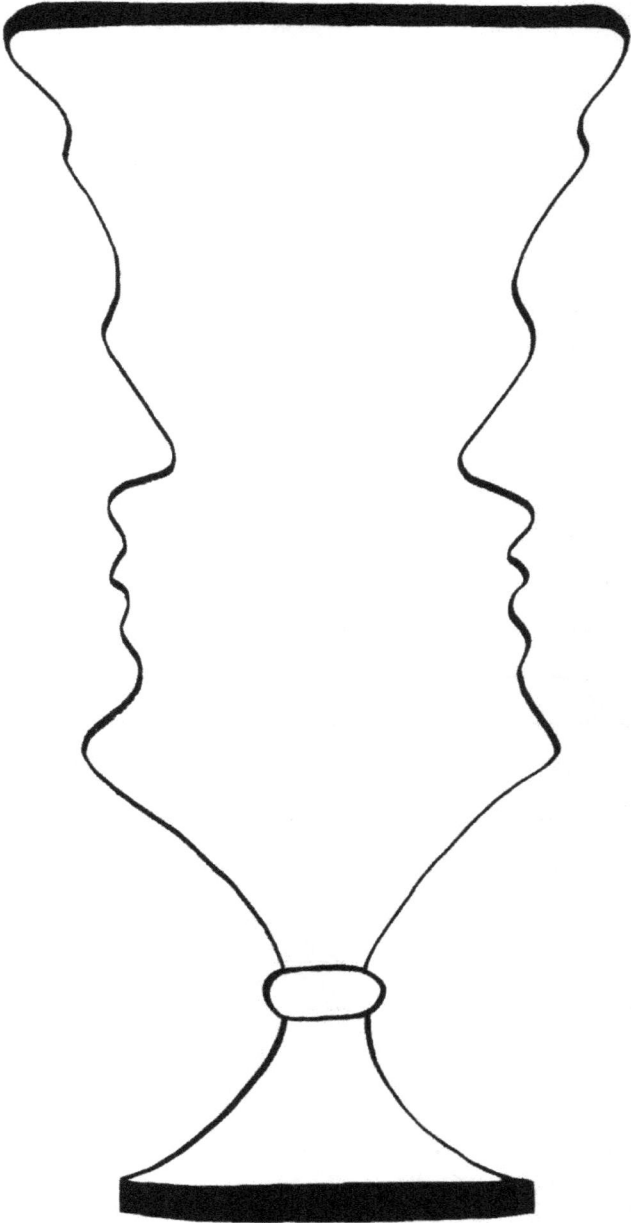

Chapter 8

GREATNESS

THE NEXT MORNING, the young warrior addressed his father with renewed energy. "Father," he said, "last night something happened..."

"What happened, my son?"

"I felt that I slept like... like a baby!"

The father laughed, "That's wonderful, son. I guess the Warrior's Prayer helped you get some much-needed rest."

"Yes! You were right again. I felt..."

The boy searched for the best word and finally said, "... secure."

"Very good, my son, very good. You know, you're not the only one who gets this type of comfort from prayer. I'm so glad for you."

"Thank you, father." The young warrior then approached his father with a concern. "Father," he said, "I was thinking..."

"Yes?"

"Is it wrong for me to try and be the greatest fighter in the land?"

"Of course not, my son. Why do you ask?"

"Because sometimes I feel that I'm being selfish by my desires for greatness."

"One is not selfish who remains forever humble. In fact, true greatness can only be achieved with humility."

"Then, is it possible to enjoy greatness once it is achieved?"

"Yes, but it is only possible if you remain humble."

"How can one be both humble and great? It just doesn't sound right."

"This is an example of the paradox of greatness, my son."

"The what of greatness?"

"Par-a-dox," said the father. "A paradox is something that is seemingly contradictory, but it is very true. Let me give you an example."

The boy was listening intently.

"It is like the driving force of life --- the yin and yang. The law of contrasting opposites; day and night, hard and soft, man and woman, and yes... greatness and humility."

"But why is this so?"

"It is so because there has to be a balance in order for life and nature to be in harmony."

"I get it," said the boy. "It is not only possible to be great and humble, but it's actually the only way, right?"

"It is the only *true* way --- that is correct."

And so, the boy joined his father for a healthy breakfast. The entire time, he thought about:

THE PARADOX OF GREATNESS:
TRUE GREATNESS CAN ONLY BE ACHIEVED
BY THOSE WHO ARE HUMBLE.

Notes

Chapter 9

FAMILY

AFTER BREAKFAST, THE YOUNG WARRIOR made an observation. "Father," he said, "you look different this morning."

"Do I?"

"Yes, you look... happy."

The father laughed aloud. "I can see you're starting to develop your sixth sense, my son. And yes, I am happy," he said as he wiped a tear from his cheek. "And you should be too."

"Why?"

"Because your mother arrives today."

The boy jumped up and down in joy. "That's great! That's wonderful! That's great AND wonderful," he shouted. "It's about time she came back, right?"

"Yes, son. But you know very well that your mother's presence was desperately needed by your grandmother."

"I know, I know," said the boy. "It's just that it seems like she was gone for a long time. And, no offense father, but mother's cooking is better."

"I agree with you, son. I enjoy your mother's meals too."

"I can't wait to show her everything I've learned! She will be impressed with my new techniques, my new footwork, and my balance."

"I'm sure your mother will be excited to see all your techniques, son."

"Father," the boy asked, "how do *you* keep your balance?"

"That's very easy, son." He put two fingers up in the air. "Two words: *your mother*."

"Mother? Is she also a fighter?"

The father laughed, "No, my son. Your mother is not a fighter per se, but she has fought very hard all her life so we can provide for you."

"Oh?" The boy was surprised. "I thought you were the one who works hard to bring us food."

"Yes, I do work hard," said the father, "but your mother also works hard. In fact, her job is just as important as mine, if not more."

"Oh, I get it," said the boy, "this is what you were talking about when you told me about the paradox of greatness, right?"

"Very good, son. Your attention to my teachings makes me proud." He continued, "You see, your mother and I are like the yin and yang; two opposites necessary to balance each other and to guide your upbringing."

"Wow," said the boy, "now I know why you're such a great father."

"Thank you, son. But, in reality, no man can be a great father without a great mother's help. And likewise, no man can achieve greatness without the love and support of a great woman."

BEHIND EVERY GREAT MAN
IS A GREAT WOMAN.

Notes

Chapter 10

STOP THE BULLET

THERE WAS A SOFT KNOCK at the door.

"Mother! It's mother!" the boy yelled.

"Ask who it is, first," advised the father. "Remember, a great warrior is always alert and ready for action."

"Who is it?" asked the young warrior, assuming a ready stance.

"Your mother."

The young warrior recognized his mother's voice and quickly opened the door. He greeted his mother with a shower of hugs and kisses. And soon, he was showing her the new skills he'd learned while she was away.

"Very impressive," she said. "I'm proud of you."

"Thank you, mother."

"Has your father taught you his technique on how to stop an arrow?"

"No," said the young warrior, "but he told me the story."

"Well sit down, both of you," she said, "and let me tell you what happened to me on my way home."

- • -

"AS I GOT CLOSE TO OUR VILLAGE, I heard several gunshots and then I saw two young men running away. They were coming in my direction. One of them had a gun in his hand. When they saw me, they stopped. The one with the gun raised it and pointed it at me."

"What did you do?" asked a stunned young warrior.

"I did what any sensible mother would have done. I told him that it's not very nice --- in fact, it's downright disrespectful --- to be pointing a dangerous weapon at a woman, let alone a mother."

"What happened next?" asked the boy.

"I said: *Now, go and take care of your own mother. Who knows? Maybe someone is pointing a gun at her this very minute just like you're doing with me.*"

"And then?" The young warrior was anxious to know.

"They ran away, calling their mother's name, I suppose."

"Were you scared?" asked the boy.

"Yes," said the mother, "but I believe they were more scared than I."

Father, mother, and son gave each other a group-hug. They were happy to be reunited and to reclaim their balance in life.

THE BEST WAY TO STOP A BULLET:
STOP IT BEFORE IT EVER LEAVES THE WEAPON!

– • –

THAT NIGHT, JUST BEFORE BEDTIME, both parents spoke to their son, the young warrior.

"Son," said the father, "I have taught you many lessons and I believe you've taught me some yourself... although you may not realize it just yet."

"What are you trying to tell me, father?"

"I'm trying to tell you that your mother and I are very proud of you and we love you, son."

"We love you," echoed the mother.

"I love you both, too."

"One day," said the mother, "your father may even teach you how to stop an arrow..."

"But for the time being," added the father, "your mother has taught you how to stop a bullet."

The young warrior smiled quietly.

He was tired.

Tired and sleepy.

"Good night, father. Good night, mother."

"Good night, son," they said in unison.

– • –

"So, YOU WANT TO KNOW HOW TO STOP A BULLET?"
asked the great warrior.

"Yes, yes!" yelled his disciples.

"Let me tell you about my mother..."

Notes

BIBLIOGRAPHY

Martial Arts Teaching Tales of Power and Paradox, P. Fauliot, Inner Traditions, Rochester, Vermont, 2000.

The Art of War, Sun Tzu, Dell Publishing, New York, NY, 1983.

Zen in the Martial Arts, J. Hyams, J.P. Tarcher, Inc., 1979.

PHOTOS

ALWAYS REACH OUT FOR HELP –

SOMEONE WILL BE THERE FOR YOU.

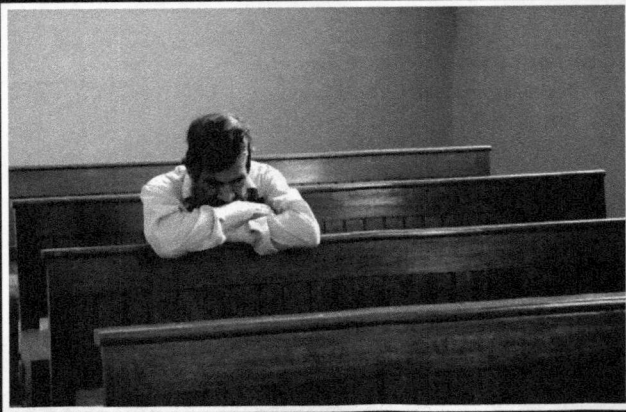

−BELIEF−

Accept the affirmations from within, and you shall succeed.

© 2011 José Luis Hinojosa

This is one of the many motivational posters
my camera helps me create.

I always tell my kids that success is simply the ABCs backwards. That is, what your mind can **c**onceive, and your heart can **b**elieve, you can **a**chieve.

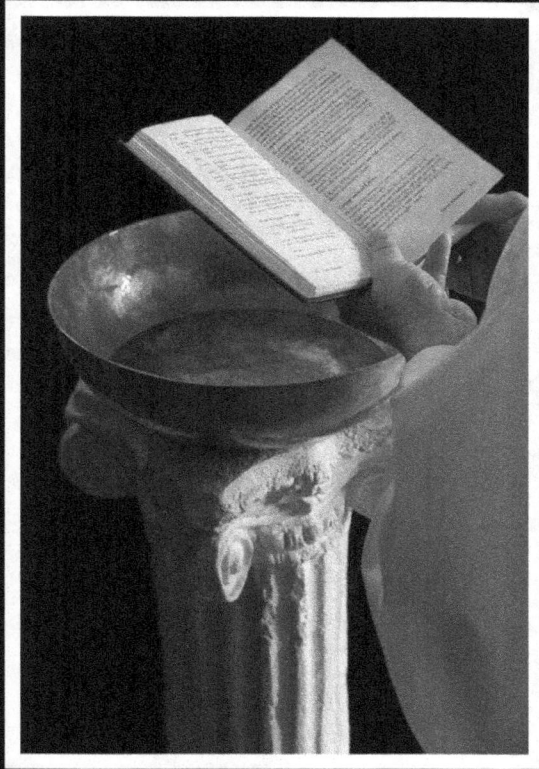

— F A I T H —

Faith can purify your soul when nothing else can.

© 2011 José Luis Hinojosa

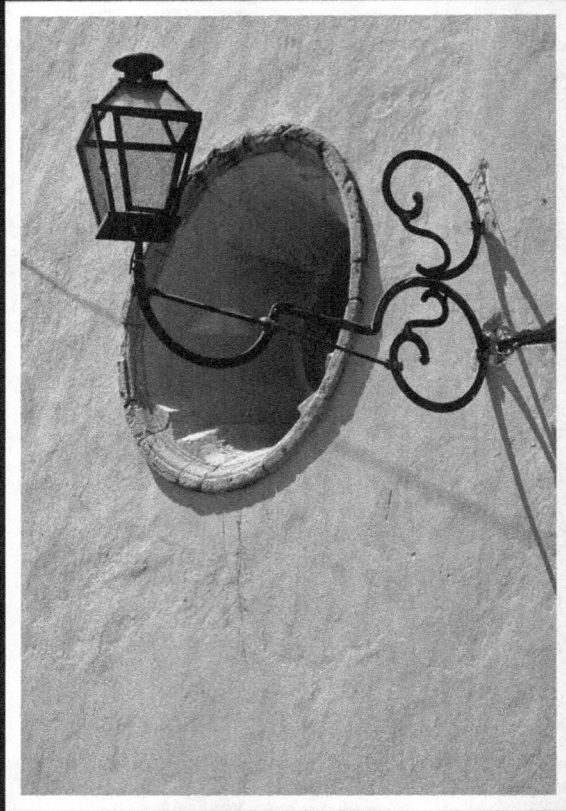

–TIMING–

When the window of opportunity is small,
let your inner light guide you toward success.

© 2011 José Luis Hinojosa

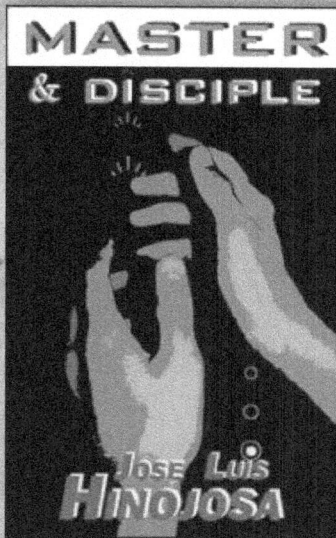

Dr. Hinojosa's grand champion ring that he won in Rosenheim, Germany in 2005… and the popular card game it inspired, Grand Champion®. The card game, just like *Master and Disciple*, teaches good moral values.

ABOUT THE AUTHOR

José Luis Hinojosa, MD and his family emigrated from Mexico to the USA when he was only 7 years old. He was fortunate to attend an Ivy League school (Brown University) for his undergraduate studies, after which he matriculated at the University of Cincinnati College of Medicine (Cincinnati, OH) to earn his Doctor of Medicine degree. After completing his specialty in Family Medicine in south Texas, he had a successful private practice for 25 years. Today, he is Chief of Staff at Stanton County Hospital and Medical Director at Stanton County Family Practice in Johnson, Kansas. Always wanting to continue learning, he will attain his Masters of Science in Healthcare Administration from Grand Canyon University in early 2016.

Besides being a physician leader, Dr. Hinojosa is also a martial arts leader. He has trained and taught the martial arts for 40 years and has won many titles, including *World Championships* in Germany and México, multiple Hall of Fame awards, including a *Lifetime Achievement Award*, and he is a crowd favorite with his powerful, creative, and highly entertaining routines – most notably, his award winning form entitled *Reflections of an Old Man*, where he dresses up as an elderly man with a cane and dazzles the crowd while reminiscing about his youth. Speaking of youth, Dr. Hinojosa has three children (JL, Laura, and Alexis) who always inspire him; he is also happily married to Maria Elena Hinojosa.

As an innovator, Dr. Hinojosa invented a fascinating medical device (patent pending) that is positioned to revolutionize health care around the globe – please go to www.TheMDMedical.com for more information on this. He also invented the popular game *Grand Champion®,* the first ever card game related to the martial arts. *Master and Disciple*, like *Grand Champion®,* teaches good moral values and became so highly-acclaimed that in 2008 Dr. Hinojosa was inducted into the Universal Martial Arts Hall of Fame as *Author of the Year* because of the teachings and lessons found in *Master and Disciple*.

This second edition of *Master and Disciple* marks the 11th book authored by Dr. Hinojosa. He is a playwright (*Rosi Milagros* – a two act play that takes place in 1924 México) and co-wrote the screenplay for an independent feature length film (*Campeón: A Journey of the Heart*). He just finished penning his first book entirely (yes, 100%) in Spanish, entitled *¡El Lenguaje de los Triunfadores!* It is the Spanish version of his highly-popular personal improvement book, *The Language of Winners!* He is currently working on the Spanish version of *Master and Disciple* and cannot wait to release it to his Spanish-speaking family, friends, and followers. For more information on how to get ahold of any of his books, please go to www.BooksByDrHinojosa.com

Dr. Hinojosa is a stage actor and has also appeared in several feature-length films. His most recent acting work was in the world premiere run (Nov. 2011 and Jan. 2012 in three south Texas cities) of *Tales of the Hidalgo Pump House*, where he played one of the lead characters, Luis Rivera, and had the opportunity to display his singing, dancing, and comedic timing; in his most recent film, he played the villain in the feature-length 2009 Warrior Pictures film *Campeón: A Journey of the Heart.*

As a professional speaker, Dr. Hinojosa is equally fluent in Spanish as he is in English keynote presentations. He shares his experiences with his audiences with such passion and clarity, that he always "connects." It is no wonder that Dr. José Luis "Jay-el" Hinojosa is highly sought out as a motivational and inspirational speaker not only in the USA, but also in México. He is a specialist in *Leadership and Success* topics, with his most popular keynotes being: *The Making of a Leader, Dream Your Way to Success, The Five Business Lessons to Learn from Breaking Boards, and Develop a World Champion Attitude.*

DID YOU ENJOY THIS BOOK?

- Parents, did this book inspire you to spend more time with your children?

- Kids, did this book help you understand your parents' lessons and teachings better?

- Would you recommend this book to your friends and loved ones?

If so, show the world that you care and order a copy of *Master and Disciple* for your friends and loved ones right now!

HERE'S HOW TO ORDER

www.BooksByDrHinojosa.com